I0789781

The Story of a Special Day
Volume 285

October 11

*The 284th day of the year (285th in leap years).
There are 81 days remaining until the end of the year.*

by Michael Dobson

Timespinner
Press

Watch for e-book editions for Kindle, e-pub devices, and other formats from your favorite online booksellers.

For more information about the series, about us, or about your special day, please email us at editor@timespinnerpress.com.

Look for other volumes in *The Story of a Special Day,* coming often. See www.timespinnerpress.com for details and for the most recent information.

Table of Contents

For the definition of "O.S.," "CE," and "BCE" used with some dates , see the section "On Names and Dates."

Cover: The morning sun reflection on the Gulf of Mexico and the Atlantic Ocean as seen from Apollo 7 — see the COVER STORY

Quote of the Day

"One of the blessings of age is to learn not to part on a note of sharpness, to treasure the moments spent with those we love, and to make them whenever possible good to remember, for time is short.
"

Eleanor Roosevelt, first lady of the United States
born October 11, 1884.

Today
in
History
THERIACA
MAGNA
October 11

Labors of the Months: October, by Simon Bening

October 11 in History

While some days of the year are more famous than others, every day of the year is filled with important, exciting, and unusual events, from religious awakenings to natural disasters, from wars to breakthroughs in technology, and from tragedy to triumph.

In this section, you'll learn about all the events that make October 11 important, including the special event that makes up our cover story. Some events you may already know about, others may be new to you, but all of them are important parts of the history of the work.

Let's explore some of the reasons why October 11 is a very special day!

A Thor-Able rocket carrying the Pioneer 1 spacecraft, the first
spacecraft launched by NASA, on October 11, 1958.

What Happened on October 11?

From the creation of great works of engineering and art, to devastating wars and natural disasters, thousands of years of history have left their mark on each and every day of the year. Here are some important events that occurred on October 11. (Items with a photo or illustration are boxed.)

1582 — With the calendar shifts caused by the adoption of the Gregorian calendar[*], the date **October 11, 1582 does not exist** in Italy, Poland, Portugal, or Spain.

1811 — The **first steam-powered ferry** begins operation, offering service between New York City and Hoboken, New Jersey.

1865 — The **Morant Bay rebellion** begins in Jamaica with a protest march against injustice and widespread poverty. The "most severe suppression of unrest in the history of the British West Indies" results in over 400 deaths and hundreds more arrests.

---

[*] The Gregorian calendar, used by most of the world today, replaced the older Julian calendar in different years in different countries. For a discussion of calendar types, see "What Day of the Week is October 11?"

1890 — The **Daughters of the American Revolution** (DAR) is founded.

1910 — Theodore Roosevelt becomes the **first US president to fly in an airplane**.

1942 — During the Guadalcanal campaign, the US and Japanese navies meet at the **Battle of Cape Esperance**, resulting in a US victory.

1954 — The **Việt Minh**, a Communist-led movement seeking independence of Vietnam from France, takes official **control of North Vietnam**.

1958 — The newly-formed US space agency NASA launches its first spacecraft, the lunar orbiter **Pioneer 1**. It fails to reach orbit. *(Photo page 6)*

1962 — The highly influential Second Vatican Council **(Vatican II)** begins; it will last until December and make numerous changes in the practice of Roman Catholicism.

Cover Story
1968 — Apollo 7 Lifts Off

The first of the Apollo missions to carry astronauts into space, Apollo 7, lifted off at 3:02 PM UTC[†] from Cape Kennedy, Florida. Commanded by astronaut Walter M. Schirra, along with astronauts Donn F. Eisele and Walter Cunningham, the ten-day mission was designed to test the procedures and systems that would be part of the eventual lunar landing mission.

Apollo 1 was intended to be the first Apollo mission into space, but a tragic launch pad fire that claimed the lives of all three astronauts resulted in a 21-month investigation along with numerous improvements in technology and procedures. During that time, several unmanned flights took place.

Apollo 7 was the first three-person American space mission, as well as the first spacecraft to include a live television broadcast. The crew practiced a simulated lunar module rendezvous and docking, as well as numerous other tests. During the mission, there was significant conflict between demands of ground control (CAPCOM) and the crew, and two of the astronauts were rejected for future missions as a result. Overall, the mission did achieve all its stated objectives, allowing Apollo 8 to achieve lunar orbit only two months later.

---

† Coordinated Universal Time (UTC) is the successor to Greenwich Mean Time (GMT), a common reference point for time zones.

1975 — The long-running and influential comedy and variety series **Saturday Night Live** premiers on NBC.

SATURDAY
NIGHT
LIVE

Saturday Night Live logo

1976 — George Washington is promoted posthumously to 6-star general (General of the Armies of the United States), on the grounds that no US military officer should ever outrank him. The 6-star rank‡ had previously been held by only one person in American history, General John J. "Black Jack" Pershing.

---

‡ Unofficial name; actual number of stars never set by law, but considered to outrank 5-star generals.

1984 — Shuttle astronaut Kathryn Sullivan performs the **first space-walk by an American woman** (3.5 hours) during a mission aboard the space shuttle *Challenger*.

Astronaut Kathryn D. Sullivan checks equipment in the open cargo bay of the space shuttle *Challenger*, October 11, 1984

1986 — The **Reykjavík Summit** between US President Ronald Reagan and Soviet General Secretary Mikhail Gorbachev begins. Although the talks themselves end in collapse, the progress begun there resulted in an important missile treaty the following year.

2000 — NASA launches *Discovery* on the **100th Space Shuttle mission**.

Quote of the Day

"If in our daily life we can smile, if we can be peaceful and happy, not only we, but everyone will profit from it."

Thích Nhât Hạnh, Buddhist monk
born October 11, 1926

Births
and
Deaths
October 11

First Lady Eleanor Roosevelt, born October 11, 1884.
Official White House portrait by Douglas Granville Chandor

Notable October 11 People

With the current world population at about seven billion people, on average about 19 million people also celebrate their birthdays on October 11 — and that isn't counting millions and millions who came before! No matter when you were born, you share your birthday with many special people whose accomplishments (and occasionally embarrassments) have been noted as part of history.

In this section, you'll meet fascinating people who share your birthday, or who died on this day in history. They're organized by what they're famous for, and then in reverse chronological order from most recent to earliest. Those who are shown in photographs or artwork have a box around them. We don't have photos of everyone, so please forgive us if your favorite person is missing.

Some of these people you've heard of, others will be new to you, but they all make up an important part of the reason that October 11 is a truly special day!

HEINZ BAKED BEANS

WITH TOMATO SAUCE.

The beans are actually BAKED, not boiled.
The quantity for each can is weighed to insure
uniform proportion of beans and sauce. No
such flavor found in any other.

SWEET PICKLES,

TOMATO KETCHUP,   TOMATO SOUP,

INDIA RELISH,   PRESERVES,

CELERY SALAD,   TOMATO CHUTNEY,

MUSTARD DRESSING.

Altogether **57** Varieties of
Pure Food Products,

Which are distributed everywhere through
our Branch Houses.

PRINCIPAL PLANT,—PITTSBURGH, U.S.A.

Advertisement for Heinz Baked Beans and other products,
originally published somewhere between 1870 and 1900.

Who Was Born on October 11?

Art and Illustration

Joe Simon, comic book writer and editor during the Golden Age of comics, known for his long partnership with Jack Kirby, in which he co-created such characters as Captain America, Sandman, and many others. He was inducted into the Will Eisner Comic Book Hall of Fame in 1999. *(1913)*

Dorothy Woolfolk, comic book writer and first female editor at DC Comics, credited with creating Superman's weakness "kryptonite." She also created and wrote the young adult mystery series featuring teen detective Donna Rockford. *(1913)*

Business and Philanthropy

Dan Evins, American entrepreneur who co-founded the Cracker Barrel chain of restaurants. *(1935)*

Henry J. Heinz, founded the H. J. Heinz Company, which popularized tomato ketchup in the US. He was a pioneer in sanitary standards for food manufacturing and in providing benefits for his employees. *(1844)*

George Williams, English draper and philanthropist who founded the Young Men's Christian Association (YMCA). *(1821)*

Government and Military

Patty Murray, first female senator from Washington State who became highest-ranking woman in the US Senate. *(1950)*

Roscoe Robinson, Jr., US Army officer who was the first African-American to achieve the rank of four-star general. *(1919)*

Roscoe Robinson, Jr., as a West Point cadet, class of 1951

Douglas Munro, received the Medal of Honor for actions during the Guadalcanal campaign of World War II; only member of the US Coast Guard to ever win that award. *(1919)*

Douglas A. Munro

Fred Trump, real estate developer best known as the father of 45th US President Donald Trump. *(1905)*

Person of the Day
Eleanor Roosevelt

First Lady of the United States, politician, diplomat, and political activist, Eleanor Roosevelt was kown as the "First Lady of the World" for her achievements in the field of human rights.

A niece of US President Theodore Roosevelt, she married future President Franklin D. Roosevelt, her fifth cousin once removed. She was integral in keeping her husband in politics after losing the normal use of his legs from polio, and was active throughout FDR's presidency.

Eleanor Roosevelt was controversial for her outspoken stand on issues of the day, particularly her advocacy of civil rights. Following FDR's death in 1945, she served as US delegate to the United Nations, where she chaired the UN Commission on Human Rights.

Widely regarded as one of the most admired women of the 20th century, Eleanor Roosevelt's legacy still shapes the role of the modern first lady. *(1884)*

Eleanor Roosevelt

Harlan F. Stone, Associate and later Chief Justice of the US Supreme Court, US Attorney-General, and dean of Columbia Law School. *(1872)*

Harlan F. Stone

Emily Davison, British suffragette arrested multiple times. She went on hunger strikes during her prison stays, and was force-fed some 49 times during her captivity. She died in a protest in which she stepped in front of the horse of King George V at the Epsom Derby. *(1872)*

Front page of the *Daily Sketch*, June 9, 1913, commemorating the death of Emily Davison

Grigory Potemkin (Григо́рий Потёмкин), Russian prince, military leader, and statesman. As governor-general of the southern provinces of Imperial Russia, he became known for the "Potemkin village," fake villages designed to show visiting officials that the lands were filled with happy, well-fed people. *(1739§)*

Grigory Potemkin

§ Potemkin was born on October 11, 1739, according to the Gregorian calendar, but at the time of his birth, Russia still used the Julian "old style" calendar (it didn't convert until 1918), so his birthday is also O.S. September 30, 1739. See "What Day of the Week is October 11?" and "On Names and Dates" for more information about different calendars.

Journalism and Letters

James M. McPherson, historian who received the 1989 Pulitzer Prize for his best selling *Battle Cry of Freedom: The Civil War Era. (1936)*

Elmore Leonard, American novelist and screenwriter known for his westerns, mysteries, and thrillers, including *Get Shorty, Mr. Majestyk,* and *3:10 to Yuma,* among many others. Named a Grand Master of the Mystery Writers of America and received the F. Scott Fitzgerald Literary Award for outstanding achievement in American literature. *(1925)*

François Mauriac, French novelist and poet who received the Nobel Prize in Literature in 1952. *(1885)*

Music

Paulette Carlson, country singer-songwriter who was founder and lead vocalist of the band Highway 101, with four No. 1 hit singles. *(1952)*

Daryl Hall, rock singer-songwriter best known as co-founder of Hall & Oates; known for such hits as "Kiss on My List," "I Can't Go for That (No Can Do)" and "Maneater." *(1946)*

Dottie West, country music singer and songwriter whose hits include "Here Comes My Baby Back Again," "Country Sunshine," and "A Lesson in Leavin'." *(1932)*

Art Blakey, jazz drummer and bandleader who co-founded the Jazz Messengers; member of the Down Beat Jazz Hall of Fame, the Modern Drummer Hall of Fame, and the Grammy Hall of Fame; received a Grammy Lifetime Achievement Award in 2005. *(1919)*

Simon Sechter, Austrian composer thought to have been the most prolific composer who ever lived, with over 5,000 fugues, five operas, and numerous masses and oratorios to his credit. He died in poverty. *(1788)*

Simon Sechter, by Joseph Kriehuber (1840)

Performing Arts

Michelle Trachtenberg, actress known for roles on *Buffy the Vampire Slayer* and *Gossip Girl*, along with such films as *Harriet the Spy* and *Inspector Gadget.* (1985)

Matt Bomer, actor best known for his role as conman and thief Neal Carrey in the TV series *White Collar.* (1977)

Emily Deschanel, actress best known for her starring role on the TV series *Bones.* (1976)

Stephen Moyer, best known for playing vampire Bill Compton in the TV series *True Blood.* (1969)

Jane Krakowski, known for such roles as Jenna in the sitcom *30 Rock* and Elaine on *Ally McBeal.* (1968)

Luke Perry, actor best known as Dylan McKay on the TV series *Beverly Hills 90210.* (1964)

Michael J. Nelson, comedian and writer best known for the cult television series *Mystery Science Theater 3000.* (1964)

Joan Cusack, actress nominated for two Academy Awards in the Best Supporting Actress category for her roles in *Working Girl* and *In & Out*; also was the voice of Jessie in the *Toy Story* franchise. (1962)

David Morse, actor first famous for playing Dr. Jack "Boomer" Morrison in the medical drama *St. Elsewhere*, along with numerous film and other television roles. (1953)

Jerome Robbins, theatrical choreographer, director, and producer of such hits as *The King and I, West Side Story, Gypsy,* and *Fiddler on the Roof. (1918)*

Religion and Philosophy

Thích Nhât Hạnh, Vietnamese Buddhist monk and peace activist nominated for a Nobel Peace Prize by Dr. Martin Luther King, Jr.; author of over 100 books. *(1926)*

Johan Oscar Smith, Norwegian Christian leader who founded the Brunstad Christian Church denomination. *(1871)*

Archbishop Jean-Baptiste Lamy, French Roman Catholic prelate who served as the first archbishop of Santa Fe, New Mexico. His life and career inspired the Willa Cather novel *Death Comes for the Archbishop. (1814)*

Samuel Clarke, Anglican clergyman and philosopher, known for his ideas on proving the existence of God as well as for his theories on rectitude. *(1675)*

Science

Friedrich Bergius, German scientist who shared the 1931 Nobel Prize in Chemistry for development of chemical high-pressure methods and the Bergius process for producing synthetic fuel from coal. *(1884)*

Sports

Steve Young, American football quarterback with the San Francisco 49ers and Brigham Young University; member of both the College Football Hall of Fame and the Pro Football Hall of Fame. *(1961)*

Maria Bueno, Brazilian tennis player who was ranked world number one female player four times; first woman ever to win all four Grand Slam double titles in one year. *(1939)*

LaVell Edwards, head football coach for Brigham Young University ranked as one of the most successful college football coaches of all time. *(1930)*

Eddie Dyer, baseball pitcher and manager *(right)* known for leading the St. Louis Cardinals to victory over the Brooklyn Dodgers in the first postseason playoff game in baseball history, then went on to defeat the favored Boston Red Sox in the 1946 World Series. *(1899)*

Meriwether Lewis, by Charles Willson Peale

Who Died on October 11?

Art and Photography

Dorothea Lange, American photojournalist best known for her Depression-era photography. *(1965)*

Military and Exploration

Lewis "Chesty" Puller, American Marine Corps general; most decorated Marine in American history. *(1971)*

Meriwether Lewis, American soldier and explorer best known as co-leader of the Lewis and Clark Expedition. *(1779)*

General Casimir Pulaski, Polish nobleman and military leader who fought in the American Revolutionary War; considered one of the fathers of the American cavalry. *(1779)* *(Photo page 32)*

Music

Werner von Trapp, member of the Trapp Family Singers; inspiration for "Kurt" in the play and film *The Sound of Music. (2007)*

Casimir Pulaski

Performing Arts

Redd Foxx, African-American comedian and actor, best known for his comedy albums and his starring role on the sitcom *Sanford and Son. (1991)*

Redd Foxx

Chico Marx, member of the Marx Brothers comedy act whose stage personal was a con artist of Italian origin. *(1961)*

The Marx Brothers (1941) From left to right: Chico Marx, Groucho Marx, and Harpo Marx

Poetry and Literature

MacKinley Kantor, American writer who received the Pulitzer Prize for his Civil War novel *Andersonville;* author of 30 novels. *(1977)*

Jean Cocteau, French writer, artist, and filmmaker known for his 1929 novel *Les Enfants Terribles* and for such films as *The Blood of a Poet* and *Orpheus*. (1963)

Sir Thomas Wyatt, English ambassador and poet credited with introducing the sonnet into English literature. *(1542)*

Sir Thomas Wyatt, by Hans Holbein the Younger

Politics

Rita Cetina Gutiérrez, Mexican educator who helped lead the first wave of feminism in that country. *(1908)*

Religion

Hans Herr, Swiss religious leader who became the first Mennonite bishop in America. His home in Lancaster, Pennsylvania, now a museum, is the oldest Pennsylvanian German settlement still in existence. *(1725)*

Huldrych Zwingli, Swiss Calvinist leader in the Protestant Reformation; helped found the Reformed faith, represented by denominations such as Presbyterian and Congregationalist churches. *(1531)*

Science

James Prescott Joule, mathematician and physicist whose studies of the nature of heat led to the development of the first law of thermodynamics; namesake of the "joule," a measure of energy. Science was his hobby; he managed the family brewery, where he converted older steam equipment into electric motors. *(1889)*

Ehrenfried Walther von Tschirnhaus, German mathematician and physicist considered by some to have invented European porcelain. *(1708)*

Sports

"Stormin'" Norman Cash, first baseman with the Detroit Tigers, known for hard living and his sense of humor. *(1908)*

James Prescott Joule, by C. H. Jeens

Quote of the Day

"We must believe in luck. For how else can we explain the success of those we don't like?"

Jean Cocteau, poet and filmmaker,
died October 11, 1963

39

 Michael Dobson

For GENERAL PULASKI MEMORIAL DAY: *Casimir Pulaski in defense of Czestochowa* by Juliusz Kossak (1883)

Holidays Around the World

If you're looking for a reason to take your special day off, you should know that every single day is a holiday somewhere in the world! Here's some of what you can celebrate on October 11!

October 11 General Events

General Pulaski Memorial Day (United States)

Each year, by Presidential Proclamation, October 11 is ceelbrated as General Pulaski Memorial Day, commemorating this Polish hero of the American Revolution. (See "Who Died on October 11?)

International Day of the Girl Child (worldwide)

The United Nations designates October 11 as a day to support opportunity for girls worldwide and to increase awareness of gender inequality faced by girls.

International Newspaper Carrier Day (worldwide)

Created by the Newspaper Association of America, International Newspaper Carrier Day is part of National Newspaper Week, and highlight the contribution newspaper carriers make in delivering the news to their neighbors. (This is not the same as Newspaper Carrier Day, observed on September 4, which honors Barney Flaherty, the first newspaper carrier/paperboy hired in the US.)

National Coming Out Day (numerous countries)

Founded in the US in 1988, this LGBTQ awareness day combats silence and ignorance about homosexuality and other non-mainstream gender identities.

Revolution Day (Republic of Macedonia)

The Republic of Macedonia celebrates Revolution Day (Ден на востанието, or *Den na vostanieto*), honoring the beginning of the anti-fascist war during World War II.

October 11 Food Holidays

In the United States, almost every day of the year is dedicated to a particular food. (Some other countries do this also, but not every day.) Sponsored by manufacturers, retailers, farmers, or simply fans, these days are often proclaimed by the President, Congress, state governors, or mayors. Given that there are more different foods than days of the year, some days honor more than one kind of food!

In the US, October 11 is **National Sausage Pizza Day**. While greasy foods definitely aren't healthy, they are quite tasty. Eat them in moderation year-around, but perhaps today is a day to splurge!

October 11 is also **Southern Food Heritage Day**. created by the Southern Food and Beverage Museum, located in New Orleans, Louisiana.

In addition, the entire month of October is used to celebrate numerous foods. Here's a list of what to eat in the month of October!

- National Apple Month
- National Applejack Month
- National Caramel Month
- National Cookie Month
- National Dessert Month
- National Pasta Month
- National Pickled Peppers Month
- National Pizza Month
- National Popcorn Poppin' Month
- National Pork Month
- National Pretzel Month
- National Seafood Month

Religious Feast Days and Holidays

Old Michaelmas Day (Celtic)

The religious holiday known as Michaelmas honors the archangel Michael, who defeated Satan in the war in heavan. In most Western Christian traditions, Michaelmas is celebrated on September 29, but .some celebrate it on October 11, the original date on the Julian calendar.**

** See "What Day of the Week is October 11?" and "On Names and Dates" for more information about different calendars.

Saint Days

Each day in the year is considered a feast day for one or more saints. They are somewhat different in western Christianity (Catholicism and many forms of Protestantism) and in eastern (Orthodox) Christianity. (Eastern "Old Calendrists" celebrate these events on the original Julian calendar date of September 28[tt].) There are many others; this is a selection.

In *Western Christianity*, it is the feast day of Saints Alexander Sauli, Andronicus, Probus, Tarachus, Aethelburh of Barking, Cainnech of Aghaboe, Gummarus, James the Deacon, Nectarius of Constantinople, Philip the Evangelist, and Pope John XXIII.

In *Eastern Orthodox Christianity*, it is also the commemoration of the Holy Apostle Philip of the Seventy Disciples, Arsacius, Sinisius, Placidia, Gratus of Oloron, Agilbert, Emilan, Eufridus, Ansilio, Juliana of Pavilly, and Bruno the Great.

Moveable and Multi-Day Events

Some events take place over a specific week or time period. Start and finish dates may vary from year to year. Some events occur on different days each year (such as "fourth Saturday of a month"). These events sometimes include or take place on October 11.

[tt] See "What Day of the Week is October 11?" and "On Names and Dates" for more information about different calendars.

Week-Long Celebrations

- Drink Local Wine Week (2nd full week)
- Earth Science Week (2nd full week)
- Emergency Nurses Week (week that includes October 14)
- National Newspaper Week (first full week in October)
- Teen Read Week (week including Columbus Day)

Movable Events

- Emergency Nurses Day (Wednesday of Emergency Nurses Week)
- National Fossil Day (Wednesday of the 2nd full week)
- World Sight Day (2nd Thursday)

October Honorary Months

Presidents, Congresses, and nations around the world issue proclamations recognizing particular months to honor certain causes. These events generally fall in October, though honorary months do come and go. Holidays established by states and nonprofit organizations are listed if verified. If not otherwise specified, all months are US. There is some variation from year to year; some celebratory months get added and others get dropped. Two places to get up to date information are the current edition of *Chase's Calendar of Events* or the website Brownielocks. Here are some honorary designations for October.

Culture

- Black History Month (UK)
- Filipino American History Month
- German American Heritage Month (September 15-October 15 in the US)
- Hispanic Heritage Month (September 15-October 15 in the US)
- Italian American Heritage Month
- LGBT History Month
- Polish American Heritage Month

Health

- American Pharmacists Month
- Brain Tumor Awareness Month (Canada)
- Breast Cancer Awareness Month
- Dental Hygiene Month
- Down Syndrome Awareness Month
- Dwarfism/Little People Awareness Month
- Dyslexia Awareness Month
- Eczema Awareness Month
- Health Literacy Month
- Healthy Lung Month
- Infertility Awareness Month
- Liver Awareness Month
- Medical Ultrasound Awareness Month
- Physical Therapy Month
- Spina Bifida Awareness Month
- Sudden Infant Death Syndrome (SIDS) Awareness Month

- World Blindness Awareness Month

Other

- Bat Appreciation Month
- Black Speculative Fiction Month
- Caffeine Addiction Recovery Month
- Church Library Month
- Class Reunion Month
- Domestic Violence Awareness Month
- Fair Trade Month
- Feral Hog Month
- Financial Planning Month
- International Walk to School Month
- National Adopt a Shelter Dog Month
- National Arts and Humanities Month

Just for Fun

Anybody can make up a holiday, and many people do! While none of these are officially recognized and some may come and go, here are a few more holidays for October 11.

- International Top Spinning Day (2nd Wednesday)
- National Bring Your Teddy Bear to Work and School Day (2nd Wednesday)
- National Food Truck Day
- National Motorcycle Ride Day (2nd Saturday)

Quote of the Day

"I'm so glad I live in a world where there are Octobers. "

Lucy Maud Montgomery
in *Anne of Green Gables*

About
the
Month
of
THER
ACC
MAGNA
October

"October" from the *Brevarium Grimani* by Simon Bening (c.1510)

October: The Tenth Month

The sweet calm sunshine of October, now
Warms the low spot; upon its grassy mould
The purple oak-leaf falls; the birchen bough
Drops its bright spoil like arrow-heads of gold.

— *"October," William Cullen Bryant*

In Latin, *octo* means eight, so it may seem odd that October is actually the tenth month! The reason goes back to the early Roman calendar, which began the new year in March. What about January and February? They didn't exist, because winter was considered a "monthless" period. Those two months didn't join the calendar until 713 BCE, pushing October from eighth to tenth in the calendar year.

Whether it's the eighth or the tenth month, October has always had 31 days. The last day of October and the last day of February end on the same day of the week in both regular and leap years.

From a seasonal point of view, October is the second month of autumn in the Northern Hemisphere and the second month of spring Down Under. October is the equivalent of April in the other hemisphere.

As an odd bit of trivia, more US presidents have been born in October than any other month: John Adams, Rutherford B. Hayes, Chester A. Arthur, Theodore Roosevelt, and Jimmy Carter.

October in Other Cultures

The month of October has different names in different languages. Some are very similar to English (octobre, oktober, etc.), while some are quite different. Some nations use calendars other than the Gregorian, and their months may overlap with October. In lunar-based calendars, such as the Islamic calendar, months move through the seasons, but many of these languages have a word for October.

Albanian: Tetor

Anglo-Saxon: Wyn-monath (wine month)

Arabic (Egypt, Sudan, Yemen): يونأغينافبرايتشرين الأأكتوبر (uktūbar)

Arabic (Levant): حزيركانوشباتشرين الأول (tishrīn al-awwal)

Arabic (Libya): الصهناالنالتمور، الثمور (at-tumūr; al-tumūr)

Arabic (Morocco, Algeria, and Tunisia): جأيفيفرأكتوبر، أوكتوبر (uktūbər; ūktūbər)

Azerbaijani: Oktyabrl

Basque: Urri

Chinese: 十月 (Cantonese: sahpyuht; Mandarin: shíyuè; Taiwanese: chap-goeh)

Croatian: Listopad

Czech: říjen

Finnish: Lokakuu

Greek: Οκτώβριος (Októbrios)

Haitian Creole: Oktòb

Hebrew: ינפברואוקטובר (ôqtôber)

Hindi: अक्टूबर (aktūbar)

Irish (Gaelic): Deireadh Fómhair mí Dheireadh Fómhair

Italian: Ottobre

Japanese (traditional calendar): 十月 (jūgatsu); 神無月 (kaminaduki)

Khoekhoe (Nama): ǂnûǁǁnâiseb

Korean: 시월 (siweol)

Lithuanian: Spalis

Manx: Jerrey-fouyir

Maori: Whiringa ā nuku

Old English: Winterfylleþ

Polish: Październik

Quechua: Kantarayki

Russian: октябрь (oktjabr')

Sardinian: Ladàmini

Scottish Gaelic: an t-Sultain

Sesotho: Mphalane

Spanish: Febrero

Swahili: Oktoba

Swazi: iMphala

Thai: Tulakhom

Turkish: Ekim

Ukrainian: жовтень (zhovten)

Vietnamese: 腩迸 (tháng mười)

Welsh: Hydref

Yiddish: פֿעברואַאָקטאָבער (oktober)

Zulu: uOkthoba

October Sayings and Superstitions

Here are some sayings and superstitions associated with the month of October.

October Weather Superstitions

Rain in October means wind in December.

When birds and badgers are fat in October, expect a cold winter.

When berries are many in October, beware a hard winter.

If ducks do slide at Hallowtide, at Christmas they will swim; if ducks do swim at Hallowtide, at Christmas they will slide.

There will always be 29 fine days in October.

If the October moon comes without frost, expect no frost till the moon of November.

Halloween Superstitions

If you see bats flying around your house on Halloween, ghosts and spirits are nearby.

If you go to a crossroads at Halloween and listen to the wind, you will learn all the most important things that will befall you during the next twelve months.

Children born on Halloween are said to have the gift of second sight, and can ward off evil spirits.

If you see a spider on Halloween night, it means the spirit of a departed loved one is watching over you.

If you ring bells on Halloween, you will chase away evil spirits.

And if you want to meet a witch, put your clothes on inside out and walk backwards on Halloween night!

October Wedding Superstitions

If in October you do marry, love will come but riches tarry.

The three luckiest months for a wedding are June, October, and December.

An October bride will be pretty, coquettish, loving, but jealous.

Married when leaves in October thin, toil and hardships for you begin.

October Symbols

Birthstones by Culture: Although a variety of birthstones have been associated with each month, the National Association of Jewelers adopted an official list of stones for each birth month. For October, the stones are *opal* and *tourmaline*.

Other stones associated with October include *aquamarine* and *coral*. There are also birthstones associated with the signs of the zodiac. For October, Libra (9/23-10/23) is associated with *chrysolite*, and Scorpio (10/24-11/21) with *beryl*.

Birth Flowers: *Calendula*, also known as *Marigold*, or Cosmos. It is associated with warmth, elegance, and devotion, as well as comfort and healing.

Birth Tree: The ancient Druids associated trees with different months of the year. For people born between September 30 and October 27, the birth tree is *ivy*. From October 28 through November 24, it is the *reed*.

"October," by Eugène Grasset

  Michael Dobson

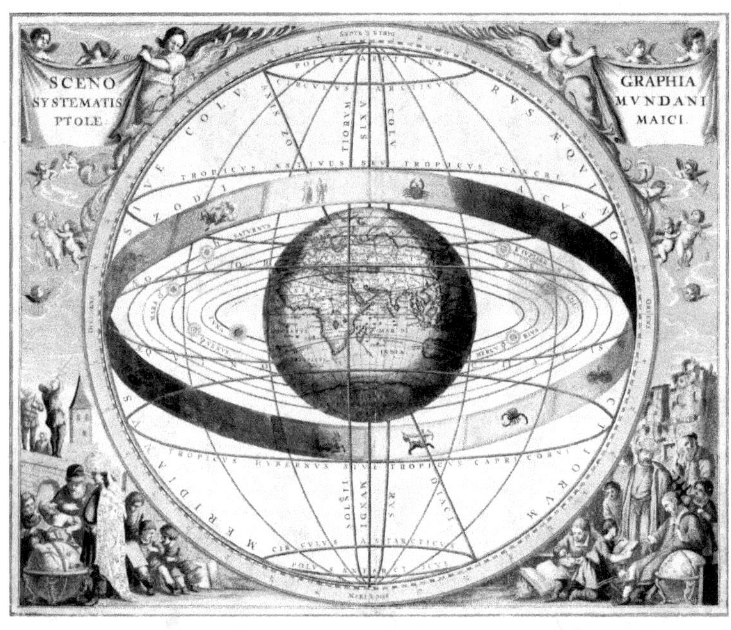

Scenography of the Ptolemaic Cosmography, by Johannes van Loon, based on Andreas Cellarius's *Harmonia Macrocosmica*, 1660

October 11 Zodiac Signs

From the perspective of someone on Earth, the Sun appears to move through the sky throughout the year, along a path astronomers call the *ecliptic plane*. The ecliptic plane is divided into twelve constellations, known as the zodiac, based on traditionally observed patterns of stars. On your birthday, you can't see your constellation, because it's in the daytime sky.

The zodiac was first developed by Babylonian astronomers about 2,500 years ago. Because they were unaware that the Earth wobbles like a spinning top (known as *precession*), they didn't make allowance for the fact that the Sun's path through the zodiac changes over time.

That means there are now two sets of dates for your birth sign. The *tropical dates* are the original Babylonian dates; the *sidereal dates* tell you where the Sun actually appears as it moves along its annual path.

For October 11, the tropical sign is **Libra** and the sidereal sign is **Virgo.**

Libra

Tropical September 23 to October 23
Sidereal October 16 to November 15

The Babylonians considered Libra, the Scales, to be sacred to the sun god Shamash, patron of truth and justice. The Romans reassigned the scales to Astraea, the celestial virgin, better known as Virgo.

Libra is symbolized by the gryphon, a mythological creature with the head, wings, and claws of an eagle and the hind legs of a lion. The Romans believed Libra was the sign "in which the seasons are balanced," and thus idolized this constellation.

Libra is an air sign, and people born under this sign are supposed to be extroverts, socially graceful, and just. Librans are supposed to be compatible with the other air signs of Gemini and Aquarius.

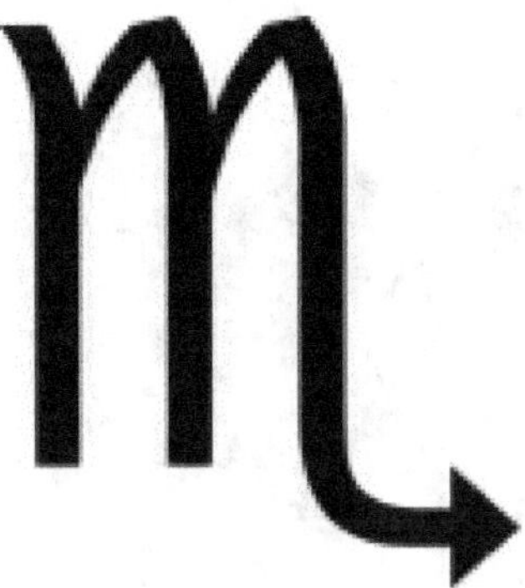

Virgo

Tropical August 23 to September 22
Sidereal September 16 to October 15

The constellation Virgo is the second-largest constellation in the night sky. Its brightest star, Spica, makes it easy to locate. If you can find the Big Dipper (Ursa Major), follow the curve in the Dipper's handle. The second bright star you see is Spica.

In Greek and Roman mythology, Virgo is associated with Demeter (Ceres), the goddess of wheat, and also with Erigone and Astraea. In astrology, Virgo is known as a "mutable sign." It's associated with being reflective and receptive to the ideas of others, sensitive to criticism, and oriented toward detail and precision.

Virgos are supposed to be compatible with Capricorn, Taurus, Cancer, and Scorpio, and to a lesser extent with Virgo and Pisces.

Illustration by Edward Penfield

What Day of the Week is October 11?

On what day of the week does October 11 fall?

Surprisingly, this isn't an easy question. Because the calendar year is 365 days long (366 in leap years), it doesn't divide evenly by the seven days of the week.

Also, the Earth goes around the Sun in about 365-1/4 days, so a calendar tends to drift over time. That's why the same date falls on different weekdays in different years.

This is made even more complicated by a change in calendars that took place in 1582. Our modern calendar has its roots in ancient Rome, in a calendar reform conducted by Julius Caesar. Caesar commissioned mathematicians to attack the problem, and they came up with the idea of leap years, and thus standardized the calendar for centuries to come. This was called the Julian calendar.

Over time, however, the small errors in Caesar's calculation compounded. That's why Pope Gregory XIII commissioned the Gregorian calendar, used in most of the world today. Some countries converted in 1582, when the calendar was first developed; some converted later; other still haven't changed.

Gregorian and Julian aren't the only types of calendars. The Hebrew year, the Islamic year, and many other calendars are used in different parts of the world and among different people.

You can convert Gregorian dates to other calendars, including the Hebrew calendar, the Islamic calendar, and even the Mayan calendar by visiting the Fourmilab Calendar Converter at http://www.fourmilab.ch/documents/calendar/.

Chinese calendar systems are quite complex and have changed several times; a full discussion is far beyond the scope of this book. If you're interested, you can find information here: http://www.hermetic.ch/cal_stud/chinese_cal.htm.

On Names and Dates

Historians use "CE" (Common Era) and "BCE" (Before the Common Era) instead of the more common "AD" (Anno Domini, or Year of Our Lord) and "BC" (Before Christ), reflecting the fact that the year-numbering system established by the Gregorian calendar is used throughout the world in many countries not culturally Christian.

The CE/BCE designation dates back to at least 1708, and has been adopted as a standard by the United Nations and the Universal Postal Union. Because this series of books covers events and people of all nations and cultures, we use the CE/BCE terms.

The abbreviation "O.S." ("Old Style") on some dates refers to the fact that the Russian Empire did not switch from the Julian to the Gregorian calendar at the same time as the rest of Europe, and therefore some figures and events have two dates.

Also, in the Julian calendar in England in the 16th century, the year began on March 25 rather than January 1. To avoid confusion with Gregorian dates, dates between January and March were often written using both years.

People and events whose original names are not in the Western alphabet have their native names (where possible) in the appropriate script shown in parenthesis. If you are using an e-reader to access an electronic version of this book, all characters don't always display on all devices.

A 50-year brass perpetual calendar.

Quote of the Day

"Time is an illusion, lunchtime doubly so."

Douglas Adams,
from *The Hitchhiker's Guide to the Galaxy*

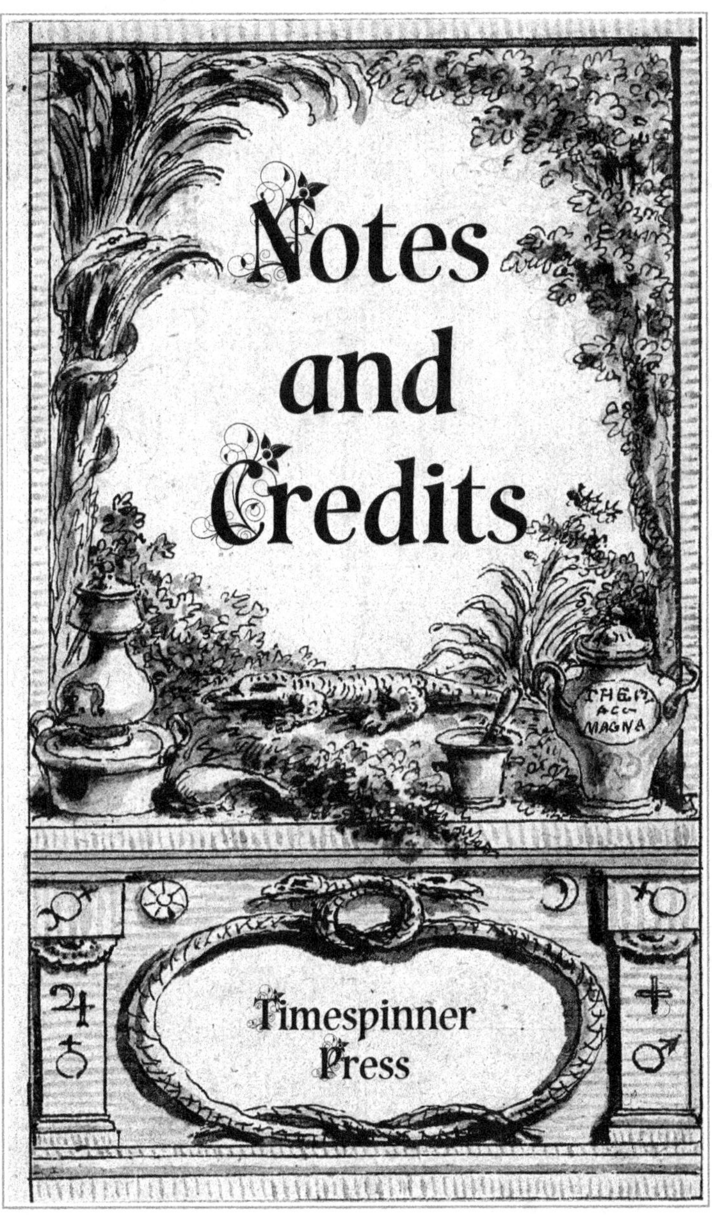
Notes
and
Credits
Timespinner
Press

Cartoon by John T. McCutcheon

Copyright, Credit, and Contact

Follow Us

Our blog "This Day in History" (http://timespinnerpress.com/this-day-in-history/) features short articles on events and people associated with each day, and updates several times each week. Also subscribe to the "Quote of the Day" at http://timespinnerpress.com/quote-of-the-day/. You can get daily links by following us on Facebook at TimespinnerPress, or on Twitter as @sidewisethinker.

Contact Us

Find an error or a format problem? Want information about the series, about us, or about when the volume for your special day might be available? Please email us at editor@timespinnerpress.com. (We also take requests if your special day isn't yet complete. Please give us at least six weeks' notice if possible.)

Sources

We owe a great debt to Wikipedia, which is our first stop for research. We attempt to make independent confirmation of all important dates and facts through a variety of other sources.

Other sources we frequently use include the Library of Congress; "on this day" listings from *Encyclopedia Britannica*, the *New York Times*, and the BBC; Omniglot for the names of months in other languages; *Chase's Calendar of Events*; and, of course, the always essential Google.

All art and photographs are either in the public domain, used under a Creative Commons license, or with a "fair use" justification, and most frequently come from Wikimedia Commons and the Library of Congress Prints and Photographs Division.

Attribution is provided where possible, or as requested by the copyright owner, or when there is particular historical significance, listed below. For information about any particular illustration or photograph, please contact us.

Credits

1. The cover photograph of the Gulf of Mexico and the Atlantic Ocean taken during the Apollo 7 mission is in the public domain as an image solely created by NASA (AS07-08-1933).

2. The illustration of the month of October used on the back cover is from the French Gothic illuminated manuscript Les Très Riches Heures du duc de Berry by the Limbourg Brothers, Jean Colombe, and an intermediate painter whose name is lost to history. It is in the public domain because its copyright has expired.

3. The box graphic used on the first page is from a 1916 pamphlet entitled "Divorce versus Democracy" authored by G. K. Chesterton, originally published in London by the Society of St. Peter and St. Paul. It is in the public domain in the US because it was published prior to 1923, and is in the public domain in all countries (including the country of origin) in which the copyright time is the author's life plus 70 years or less.

4. The graphic design for the section pages in this book is from a design originally created for a pharmacy label. It is courtesy of Wellcome Images (ICV No 11073, photo V0010813), and is used here under CC BY-SA 4.0.

5. The painting "October," from *Labors of the Month* by Simon Bening, was originally published in the first half of the 16th century, and is in the public domain because its copyright has expired.

6. The photograph of the Pioneer 1 spacecraft launch is from "Great Images in NASA," created October 11, 1958. It is in the public domain as a work created by NASA.

7. The Apollo 7 logo is in the public domain as a work created by NASA.

8. The Saturday Night Live logo only consists of simple geometric shapes or text. It does not meet the threshold of originality needed for copyright protection, and is therefore in the public domain.

9. The NASA photograph of the space walk of astronaut Kathryn D. Sullivan is in the public domain as a work created by NASA.

10. The official White House portrait of Eleanor Roosevelt by Douglas Granville Chandor is in the public domain because it was first published in the US between 1923 and 1977 without a copyright notice.

11. The advertisement for Heinz Baked Beans is in the public domain because it was first published prior to January 1, 1923.

12. The photograph of Roscoe Robinson, Jr., is in the public domain as a work created by a soldier or employee of the US Army as part of that person's official duties.

13. The photograph of Douglas Munro is in the public domain as a work created by a service member or employee of the US Coast Guard as part of that person's official duties.

14. The 1933 portrait of Eleanor Roosevelt is from the Library of Congress Prints and Photographs Division, digital ID cph. 3c08091. It is in the public domain because it was published in the US between 1923 and 1963, and although there may or may not have been a copyright notice, the copyright was not renewed.

15. The 1929 photograph of Harlan F. Stone is by Underwood & Underwood, and is from the Library of Congress Prints and Photographs Division, digital ID cph.3a38659. According to the Library of Congress, all Underwood & Underwood images are in the public domain due to expiration or lack of renewal.

16. The front page of the *Daily Sketch* for June 9, 1913, is in the public domain in the US because it was first published prior to January 1, 1923.

17. The 1847 portrait of Grigory Potemkin is in the public domain because its copyright has expired. The artist is unknown.

18. The 1840 lithograph of Simon Sechter by Joseph Kriehuber is in the public domain because its copyright has expired.

19. The 1921 photograph of Eddie Dyer is in the public domain because its copyright has expired.

20. The circa 1807 portrait of Meriwether Lewis by Charles Willson Peale is in the public domain because its copyright has expired.

21. The 1839 lithogreaph of Casimir Pulaski by James Hopwood is in the public domain because its copyright has expired.

22. The 1966 publicity photo of Redd Foxx is in the public domain because it was first published in the US between 1923 and 1977 without a copyright notice. Traditionally, publicity photographs are not copyrighted because of the way they are intended to be used.

23. The 1948 photograph of the Marx Brothers is by Yousuf Karsh, and is from the collection of the Bibliothèque et Archives Canada, image PA- 207445. It is in the public domain in Canada because it is a photograph created prior to January 1, 1949.

24. The 1812 portrait of Sir Thomas Wyatt by Hans Holbein the Younger is in the public domain because its copyright has expired.

25. The 1882 engraving of James Joule by C. H. Jeens is in the public domain because its copyright has expired.

26. The 1883 painting of Casimir Pulaski by Juliusz Kossak is in the public domain because its copyright has expired.

27. The painting "October" is from the Brevarium Grimani, circa 1510, and is in the public domain because its copyright has expired.

28. The 1815 woodcut of a proposal is in the public domain because its copyright has expired.

29. The 1896 drawing "October" by Eugène Grasset is in the public domain because its copyright has expired.

30. The celestial sphere is from Scenography of the Ptolemaic Cosmography, by Johannes van Loon, based on Andreas Cellarius's Harmonia Macrocosmica, 1660. It is in the public domain because its copyright has expired.

31. The 1906 automobile calendar is by Edward Penfield, and is in the collection of the Library of Congress Prints and Photographs Division. It is in the public domain because its copyright has expired.

32. The 50-year perpetual calendar photograph is in the public domain.

33. The cartoon by John T. McCutcheon is from his 1905 collection *The Mysterious Stranger and Other Cartoons by John T. McCutcheon*. It is in the public domain because its copyright has expired.

License Description and Terms

Aside from material purely in the public domain, photographs and other material in this book are used under specific licenses permitting free use, usually with an attribution requirement. For full text and terms of these licenses, click or enter the appropriate links below. If you believe there is an error in the copyright status or attribution of any of these images, please email us.

- Creative Commons Attribution 2.0 Generic (CC-BY 2.0): http://creativecommons.org/licenses/by/2.0/deed.en

- Creative Commons Attribution-Share Alike 3.0 Generic (CC-BY-SA 3.0): http://creativecommons.org/licenses/by-sa/3.0/

- Creative Commons Attribution-Share Alike 2.5 Generic (CC-BY-SA 2.5): http://creativecommons.org/licenses/by-sa/2.5/deed.en

- Creative Commons Attribution-Share Alike 2.0 Generic (CC-BY-SA 2.0): http://creativecommons.org/licenses/by/2.0/deed.en

- Creative Commons Attribution-Share Alike 1.0 Generic (CC-BY-SA 1.0): http://creativecommons.org/licenses/by-sa/1.0/deed.en

- CC0 1.0 Universal (CC0 1.0) Public Domain Dedication (CC0 1.0) http://creativecommons.org/publicdomain/zero/1.0/deed.en

- GNU Free Documentation License (GFDL): http://en.wikipedia.org/wiki/Wikipedia:Text_of_the_GNU_Free_Documentation_License

- License Art Libre (Free Art License): http://artlibre.org

Timespinner
Press

Other Books from Timespinner Press

The Story of a Special Day

Michael Dobson

A series of (eventually) 366 volumes covering everything that happened on your special day! Events, births, deaths, quotes, holidays, and much more. It's like a birthday card they'll never throw away!

US$7.95 print / US$2.99 ebook.

From Plassey to Pakistan

Humayun Mirza

The history of British Colonial India and the formation of Pakistan from the unique perspective of the son of Pakistan's first president and last of the royal line of Bengal, Bihar, and Orissa! This unique historical document tells the inside story of this distinguished family, including the detailed story of the coup that toppled his father from power!

US$27.95 print

A Whole New Navy: America's War in the Pacific

Miles Durr

The most comprehensive and detailed description of America's naval war in the Pacific ever—every battle, every ship, every task force and every task group from Pearl Harbor through the Japanese surrender! A must-have for the collection of every World War II buff!

US$29.95 print

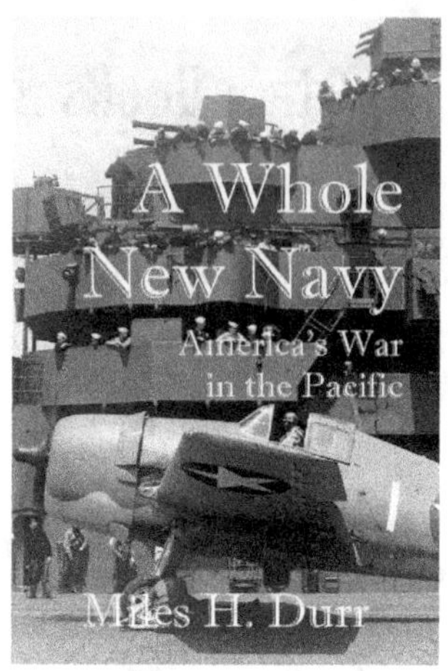

Improbable History: The Weird, the Obscure, and the Strangely Important

edited by Michael Dobson

From the birth of Western civilization to the rescue of Apollo 13, from the Leaning Tower of Pisa to Florence's Duomo, history has often turned on small, improbable details. Whatever happened to the ancient Samaritan people? Why did a fortuitous rainstorm allow the British to conquer India? How did an air raid in Italy lead to the development of chemotherapy? What happened when Albert Einstein met Adolf Hitler on the streets of Berlin? How did the Japanese manage to attack the US mainland using balloons? A cast of award-winning writers tackle some of the strangest tales in history!

US$19.95 print

The Letters of William Philip Schwartz 1842-1855

edited by John F. Schwartz

The 19th century soldier and adventurer William Philip Schwartz wrote a series of vivid and detailed letters chronicling his adventures in the Indian Wars, the Mexican-American War, the Gold Rush, and his term as Marine sergeant aboard the USS Constellation. A pioneer in photography, he took *the first known war photographs*. An unforgettable first-hand look into life in the 19th century!

US$17.95 print